A PLUME BOOK

GENE SIMMONS IS A POWERFUL AND ATTRACTIVE MAN

Julie Bergonz

Christina Vitagliano is the founder of Monster Mini Golf. She created, designed, and is responsible for a nationwide franchised chain of indoor, glow-in-the-dark, monster-themed mini golf family entertainment centers. She lives in Las Vegas and has never slept with Gene Simmons.

GENE SIMMONS

IS A POWERFUL AND ATTRACTIVE MAN

And Other Irrefutable Facts

CHRISTINA VITAGLIANO

Illustrated by Corey Marier and Craig Marier
Foreword by Gene Simmons

A PLUME BOOK

Published by the Penguin Group
Penguin Group (USA) LLC
375 Hudson Street
New York, New York 10014

USA | Canada | UK | Ireland | Australia | New Zealand | India | South Africa | China
penguin.com
A Penguin Random House Company

First published by Plume, a member of Penguin Group (USA) LLC, 2015

Illustrations by Corey Marier and Craig Marier

 REGISTERED TRADEMARK—MARCA REGISTRADA

LIBRARY OF CONGRESS CATALOGING-IN-PUBLICATION DATA
Vitagliano, Christina, author.
Gene Simmons is a powerful and attractive man : and other irrefutable facts / Christina Vitagliano ; illustrated by Corey Marier and Craig Marier ; foreword by Gene Simmons.
pages cm
ISBN 978-0-14-218162-1 (pbk.)
1. Simmons, Gene, 1949—Humor.   2. Rock musicians—United States—Humor.   I. Marier, Corey, illustrator.   II. Marier, Craig, illustrator.   III. Simmons, Gene, 1949—writer of supplementary textual content.   IV. Title.
ML420.S5629V58 2015
782.42166092—dc23   2014037614

Printed in the United States of America
10   9   8   7   6   5   4   3   2   1

Set in Tungsten
Designed by Daniel Lagin

I would like to dedicate this book to people with the willingness to survive and persevere but most of all, laugh. I was lucky enough to be born with a sense of humor and wit and this particular trait has gotten me through some pretty rough times. I am not sure where I would be without the ability to laugh.

People come in all sizes, shapes, creeds, and colors, and I have met good and bad in all. This crazy ride we call life has led me to meeting the human specimen known to be Gene Simmons, and while I would normally use the old cliché "don't judge a book by its cover" I would have to say in this case, please do!

ACKNOWLEDGMENTS

Like everything else in in our crazy lives, this book came to be with just one simple sentence that escaped from my head and fell out of my mouth. To this day my husband fears whenever I blurt out, "Hey, I have an idea!"

So with that being said, I would like to thank my husband, Patrick Vitagliano, for not only putting up with me but also being there throughout this book whenever I said, "Hey, I'm stuck and need your help." (Which, I may add, after the first hundred or so Gene-isms was quite often!)

I would like to also thank Patrick for contributing to Gene-tionary definitions and for putting up with the overabundance of the subject of Gene Simmons in our lives while I was writing this.

A big thanks to Sorche Fairbank, Ryan Sweikert, and Matthew Frederick at Fairbank Literary Representation, who helped take this from idea to book, and a thanks to Sorche for dealing with . . . me. And to Victoria Sanders for recommending Fairbank Literary.

A huge thank-you to Misty Erikson, Zenon Obuchowsky, and Mikey Ramone for helping me out with acquiring KISS fan lines and Gene Simmons facts in general.

And a big thanks to Bree Dergence and the entire staff at KISS by Monster Mini Golf for helping gather answers from little kids' surveys on Gene.

A profound thank-you to this book's editor, Becky Cole. Her enthusiasm, sharp eye, and sense of humor made all the difference. And a shout-out to her team at Penguin Group, from the talented designer Daniel Lagin to Becky's assistant, Matthew Daddona, to copy editor Brandon Hopkins, to the enthusiastic sales, publicity, and marketing staff. A huge thanks to all.

And last but not least, there are no words to describe the gratitude I have for Corey and Craig Marier, the wonder twins. They are responsible for all of the illustrations in the book. They put up with my editing, suggestions, and changes with no ego, and that to me is priceless. They have been artists with us at Monster Mini Golf for almost a decade, and to this day I believe we are blessed to have them as part of our team.

CELEBRITY FOREWORD

I have known Gene Simmons for a _very_ long time. Over
the years I have witnessed astounding feats, met incredible people, and
seen amazing places, but none so astounding, incredible, or amazing as
Gene Simmons himself.

I can remember Gene as a young boy in his early teens on the streets of
New York City. Even then, I could see Gene's inner greatness just itching to
be released. Like all kids in their early teen years, Gene was trying to be
tough, but he was new to this country, landing here at only eight years old
from Israel with his mom, and he hadn't quite found his footing. Still, it was
clear Gene Simmons, formerly called Chaim Witz, was not your average boy.
This was a boy who prior to arriving in America already had one successful
business venture behind him. At six years old, he learned to pick cactus fruit,
de-thorn it, chill it, and sell it to weary workers on the warm bus ride home
from a long day of work. He earned enough to buy his own lunch each day,
and gave the rest to his mother to help with the household expenses.

Gene continued to grow, and he not only learned the ins and outs of living in this fine country but took it a few steps further and became an American icon. How many people can call themselves a legend? Gene Simmons can, and does.

I think Gene Simmons planned on being a success the moment he launched himself out of his mother's womb. Gene had early aspirations of being a rabbi and along the way became an accomplished schoolteacher and even worked for *Vogue*. But his mission to become a megastar soon eclipsed all else. As fate would have it, one single night of television lit that spark.

As it was for most boys his age, TV was an important part of his life, and one night back in the late sixties, while watching an episode of *The Ed Sullivan Show*, Gene witnessed four skinny boys with moppy hair singing their hearts out. Young Gene was completely engaged by the band, but more important to him was what happened *after* the band stopped singing. Girls. Throngs of girls were shaking and crying and screaming in ecstasy. It was at that exact moment that Gene Simmons made the decision to become a Rock God. And it was for one reason and one reason only . . . girls.

Gene Simmons was going to get girls. In fact, Gene Simmons was going to get *all* of the girls. So it's fair to say that Ed Sullivan is to blame for the 5,000 or so women that Gene Simmons has slept with to date.

Now I look at Gene Simmons, a sixty-plus-year-old man with the energy and vitality of a teenager, with four decades of Rock Godliness behind him, and think, he is *exactly* the living legend he always knew he would be.

He is a rock star, he's acted in movies and appeared in international commercials, and only Gene Simmons could have starred in a TV series titled *Gene Simmons Family Jewels*. But Gene Simmons did not stop there. Why would he? He's a machine of perpetual energy. He is the trademarker of all trademarkers. He has trademarked his name, his signature, his basses, and his costumes. And as far as businesses and ventures go, it appears there is no stopping in sight.

Who among us could possibly fault him for having an ego?

What I find most amazing and unique is that with all of this greatness, attention, egotism, Rock Godliness, and general living legend–ness, Gene Simmons has the ability to poke fun at himself, and that, my friends, is what makes him even greater than he already appears to be.

To this day I am still Gene Simmons's closest friend, ally, admirer, and confidant. In fact, I am Gene Simmons's biggest fan. So I can say with complete confidence that even now, Gene's best is still yet to come.

You know what the best thing about Gene Simmons is? That there will only ever be one Gene Simmons. It's been the honor of a lifetime knowing him.

Sincerely,

Gene Simmons

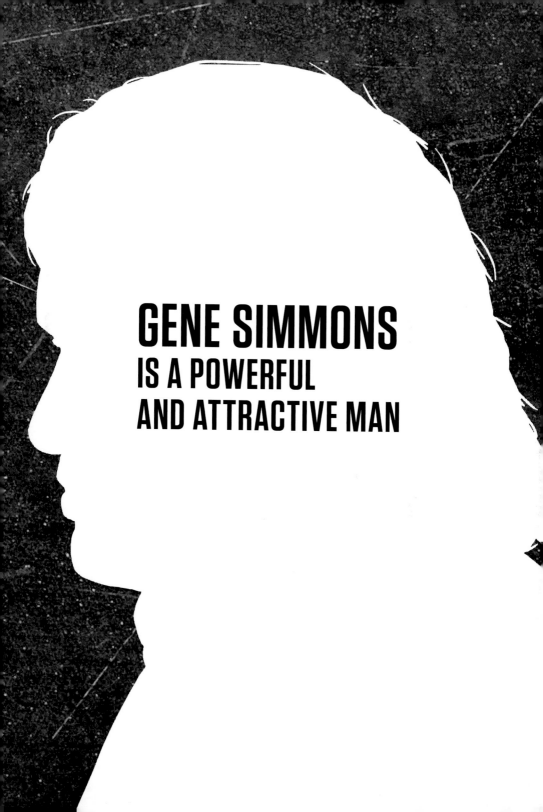

The Army's "Be All You Can Be" was inspired by Gene Simmons.

The earth revolves around the sun, the sun revolves around Gene Simmons, and Gene Simmons revolves around nothing.

When Gene Simmons puts a seashell up to his ear, he hears himself.

The Incredible Hulk is green from being envious of Gene Simmons.

Gene Simmons once scribbled down a grocery list for his assistant. It spent twenty-six weeks on the *New York Times* bestseller list.

Gene Simmons does not need a toaster; bread gladly sets itself on fire for him.

To burn off one plain M&M candy, you need to walk the full length of a football field . . . or spend five seconds with Gene Simmons.

Nestlé's 100 Grand Bar used to be called the 100 Dollar Bar, until Gene Simmons was photographed eating one.

Gene Simmons *can* always get what he wants, and does.

Before Gene Simmons, fireflies were just flies.

When Gene Simmons walks into a strip club, the girls pay *him*.

Gene Simmons is the reason Mick Jagger "can't get no satisfaction."

Straight from the Demon's Tongue

"Walk amongst the natives by day, but in your heart be Superman."

—GENE SIMMONS

Gene's ego is so big he has to step into pullover shirts.

Gene Simmons does very few motivational speaking dates because he has to coordinate his schedule with both his penis and his tongue, who both tour separately on the motivational speaking circuit.

Gene Simmons slept with Mother Nature. The 9.2 Sumatra earthquake was her orgasm.

Gene Simmons's personal sushi chef is Aquaman.

Gene Simmons has never seen a red light.

Gene Simmons can get to the center of a Tootsie Pop in one lick.

Who is Gene Simmons?

HE Is a DragOn. (Kedla, age 5)

He is a super awesome guy who wears spandex with beads and lots of makeup...he really should go for a more natural look.   (Micah, age 10)

A guy my Mom loves. (Emile, age 6)

A guy who sticks his tongue out at girls.

(Bobby, age 9)

Most rock stars travel by tour bus. . . . Gene Simmons travels in the Death Star.

Gene Simmons taught Godzilla how to breathe fire.

Eeny, Meeny, Miny, Moe

Eeny, meeny, miny, moe,

Catch the Demon by the toe.

When he hollers, then you'll know,

You shouldn't play where wild things go.

Straight from the Demon's Tongue

"My hero is me.

Why?

Because I was a poor little kid who was told,

'Hey, stupid, can't you speak English?'

Now all those people work for me."

—GENE SIMMONS

Gene Simmons can break Murphy's Law.

Groucho Marx said, "All people are born alike—except Democrats and Republicans." Gene Simmons says, "All people are born alike—except Gene Simmons."

Gene Simmons is the exception to most rules.

Gene Simmons's Escalade houses a Starbucks and a 7-Eleven.

Gene Simmons is impervious to STDs, but many STDs have come down with Gene Simmons.

Under pressure from fans, Facebook was forced to change the "Like" button on Gene Simmons's page to "Love."

One drop of Gene Simmons's sweat can cure cancer, but you can't afford it.

Gene Simmons once got a pimple, which upon closer examination turned out to be a tiny active volcano.

Bigfoot once pissed off Gene Simmons; to this day Bigfoot is still on the run.

God has a "footprints in the sand" poster to remind him of all the times that Gene Simmons had to carry him.

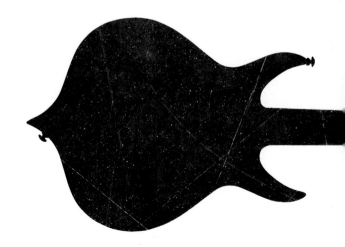

Little-known fact: The 1994 LA earthquake was caused by Gene Simmons

Who is Gene Simmons?

He is the lead singer of the oldest rock band that is touring.

(Samantha, age 11)

A guy that likes to kiss and sometimes fly. (Lauren, age 4)

SOME GIANT GUY WITH lots of black HAIR THAT dANCES ON StaGE.

(Denise, age 10)

he is the main rock man Of kiss.

(George, age 7)

I really have no idea.

(Arthur, age 13)

Gene Simmons can get not only blood from a stone but money, too.

The idea for the movie *Anaconda* originated when the director witnessed Gene Simmons peeing in the jungle.

Gene Simmons once bit the head off of Sharon Osbourne.

On the first day, Gene Simmons farmed the whole project out to God. He then took it easy for the next six days and still cleared a 35 percent profit.

Ivory soap is 99.44 percent pure. Gene Simmons is 99.44 percent impure.

Gene Simmons dyes his hair black because his real hair is solid gold.

Donald Trump is Gene Simmons's apprentice.

Jesus follows Gene Simmons on Twitter.

You Know You're a Gene Simmons Fan When . . .

- You add a second floor to your house just for your KISS collection.

- You need a rider on your homeowner's insurance policy to cover your KISS collection.

- You spend $1,900 on a tattoo of Gene's face.

- You take the KISS toys off your desk at work, and everyone assumes you were fired.

- You start using Gene phrases like "You're a powerful and attractive man" and "That's a big word, like *gymnasium*."

- You're more excited over Hello Kitty's new KISS collection puppets than your five-year-old daughter is.

Truth Be Told . . .

Gene Simmons shares a birthday with Judas Priest front man Rob Halford, singer-songwriter Billy Ray Cyrus, and current Def Leppard guitarist Vivian Campbell.

Gene Simmons once played in a band named Bullfrog Beer.

Gene Simmons has his own wine in production called "Genie in a Bottle."

Bruce Lee was so fast they had to slow the film down to see his moves, and in between each of those moves they saw Gene Simmons going to the bank.

Straight from the Demon's Tongue

"I want to do everything. I want to be the president,
I want to learn Tae Kwon Do, I want to climb mountains.
I'm always bugged by the notion that I can't do everything."

—GENE SIMMONS

Gene Simmons knows what's under the Statue of Liberty's gown.

Gene's bathroom is bigger than your house.

Dollar bills are made out of 95 percent paper and 5 percent Gene Simmons's saliva.

A Gene Simmons action figure was originally cast for the movie *Toy Story*, but there were too many issues on the set with Bo Peep.

Gene Simmons had sex with Christie Brinkley on Chuck Norris's Total Gym.

Once a year Gene Simmons delivers presents to Santa. In return Santa leaves Gene Simmons some milk and cookies.

Gene Simmons once stole Christmas from the Grinch.

Little Miss Muffet

Little Miss Muffet sat on a tuffet

Eating her curds and whey.

Along came Gene Simmons and

sat down beside her and . . . well . . .

In case of emergency, Gene Simmons's tongue can be used as a flotation device.

How did Gene Simmons learn to breathe fire?

From a meteor falling to earth. (Brian, age 8)

He swallowed a match. (Jennifer, age 7)

He looked it up on the internet. (John, age 7)

He YouTube'd it. (Willie, age 9)

By eating the KISS Hot Sauce. My Mom won't let me taste ours. (Joey, age 8)

He had lessons from a professional magician or something. (Rachel, age 10)

Straight from the Demon's Tongue

"I fail all of the time.
   It means nothing."

—GENE SIMMONS

The largest recorded snowflake was fifteen inches wide and eight inches thick, and it was still smaller than Gene Simmons's tongue.

When Paul McCartney sang "Got to Get You into My Life," it wasn't about marijuana; it was about Gene Simmons.

Seventy-five percent of Japanese women own vibrators. Gene Simmons does not live in Japan.

While in the womb, Gene Simmons frequently ordered room service and threw lavish soirees.

Gene Simmons could make Cher turn back time.

WHY DO YOU WEAR THAT STUPID BUNNY SUIT?

WHY DO YOU WEAR THAT STUPID DEMON SUIT?

Gene Simmons once beat Sylvester Stallone at arm wrestling using only his tongue.

It's Raining, It's Pouring

It's raining, it's pouring;

The rock scene was boring.

'Til Gene Simmons sung,

Stuck out his tongue,

And now the fans are soaring!

Gene be nimble,

Gene be quick,

Gene picked up your brother's chick.

Truth Be Told . . .

There is a Gene Simmons US postage stamp.

Coca-Cola put Gene Simmons's face on their bottles in France.

To promote a season of his reality show, *Gene Simmons Family Jewels*, Gene Simmons allowed his face to be affixed to talking urinal cakes in bathrooms around New York City.

When Gene Simmons breaks a sweat, everyone scrambles to put it back together.

Stan Lee was going to make Gene Simmons a superhero, but decided to stick to fiction.

Gene Simmons gives Viagra a boner.

When Gene Simmons goes swimming, he doesn't get wet; the water gets Gene Simmons.

Gene Simmons's urine is being considered as an alternative to fossil fuels.

Scientists have determined that having the "guilty feeling" gene may damage your immune system. Gene Simmons is the healthiest man on the planet.

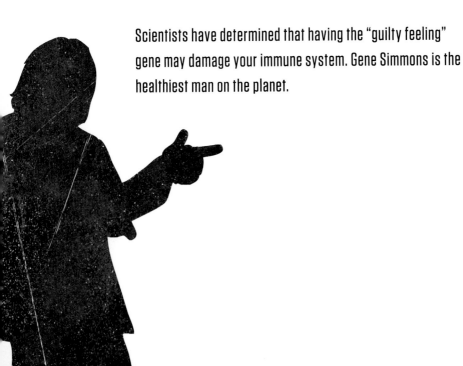

Gene Simmons can turn coal into diamonds by squeezing his butt cheeks.

Friday the 13th is afraid of Gene Simmons.

The Shroud of Turin was the single most studied artifact in human history . . . until Gene Simmons was born.

Gene Simmons once ordered osso buco at McDonald's, and they made it for him.

The Amazing Spider-Man was known as "Spider-Dude" prior to consulting Gene Simmons.

When you look in any mirror, you'll see Gene Simmons's reflection.

Woodstock was Gene's idea. He used hippies to test market it because hippies are cheap.

Gene Simmons gives Stephen King nightmares.

Jack and Jill

Jack and Jill went up the hill

To fetch a pail of water.

Jack went home and Gene banged Jill,

And now they have a daughter.

Before Gene Simmons, firecrackers were just crackers.

Jesus walked on water . . . but only once.

Never ask what Gene Simmons can do for you, but *always* ask
what you can do for Gene Simmons.

Gene Simmons makes coffee nervous.

Gene Simmons does not read his horoscope because he already
knows his day will be awesome.

Superman played with Gene Simmons action figures as a boy.

Gene Simmons doesn't need an umbrella because rain knows better.

IF GENE SIMMONS STARRED IN
THE MOVIE *THE TERMINATOR*

SIMMONS

THE
SPERMINATOR

Straight from the Demon's Tongue

"Anyone who tells you they got into rock 'n' roll for reasons other than sex, fame, and money is full of shit."

—GENE SIMMONS

The Creepy Crawly Simmons

The creepy crawly Simmons spit blood upon the stage.

Out came the fans to see creepy Simmons rage.

Then some guy in the crowd went totally insane.

And the creepy crawly Simmons left on his private plane.

What was Gene Simmons before he was a rock star?

He was a weirdo. (Becky, age 7)

He sold french Fries. (Kelly, age 7)

He was in the circus. (Peter, age 8)

He was a typer and a 6th grade student. (Ann, age 11)

AN ICE CREAM MAN. (Danny, age 6)

Gene Simmons knows what you are thinking, because it
was his idea to begin with.

Gene Simmons can beat you at tic-tac-toe in one move.

Smokey the Bear and Gene Simmons are archenemies.

Every time Gene Simmons ejaculates, an angel gets its wings.

A male emperor moth can smell a female emperor moth up
to seven miles away. It's got nothing on Gene Simmons.

Gene Simmons could get laid on the moon.

Straight from the Demon's Tongue

"I'm not delusional enough to think that what
I do is important to life as we know it.
But neither is what you do."

—GENE SIMMONS

Gene Simmons hates Volkswagen . . . as Gene Simmons will never "Think Small."

How did Gene Simmons learn to breathe fire?

He was born from a dragon?

(Jason, age 8)

a magician taught him. (Alese, age 9)

Probably after he was married because women will do that to you! (Micah, age 13)

Probablee from his weird friends.

(Devon, age 10)

He ate something "really" spicy. (Justin, age 7)

From eating tons of BBQ'd potato chips. (Mason, age 11)

Gene Simmons used to walk God to school.

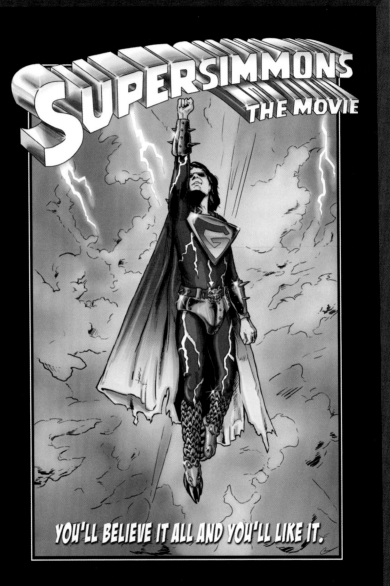

SUPERSIMMONS
THE MOVIE

YOU'LL BELIEVE IT ALL AND YOU'LL LIKE IT.

Nothing on Gene Simmons will shrink as he gets older. Especially not his head.

Jerry Lee Lewis came up with "Great Balls of Fire" after he met Gene Simmons in a locker room.

Your Gene Simmons doll got your sister's Barbie doll pregnant.

Gene Simmons is the beef Wendy's was looking for.

Gene Simmons's penis is a fairly proficient bass player.

Gene's head is so big that when it rains his clothes don't get wet.

Gene Simmons's tarot cards read, "It's good to be Gene Simmons."

When Gene Simmons plays rock-paper-scissors, ROCK always wins.

Straight from the Demon's Tongue

"I worship scones and danishes. If I never had another meal, I wouldn't care as long as I could eat pastries and jelly doughnuts."

"Sugar-free ice pops are an invention of God. I eat about fifteen pops every two days."

"I tolerate food. I love desserts. I've never met anybody who's ever had a dream about celery."

"I have had repeated dreams of being stuck in a chair with my hands tied behind my back in a cake house, and of course the only way out is to eat."

"My favorite dessert is the next one. I'm a dessert junkie."

—GENE SIMMONS

The sun does not rise until Gene Simmons gives his OK.

Gene Simmons has a yacht . . . in his swimming pool.

Gene Simmons has never fallen, and he can always get up.

Gene Simmons once stepped on a crack and broke its mother's back.

Gene Simmons doesn't wear platform shoes. They carry him voluntarily.

Gene Simmons wears sunglasses for *your* protection.

By the year 2085, 98 percent of the world's population will be direct descendants of Gene Simmons.

Straight from the Demon's Tongue

"I think I know it all, relatively speaking."

—GENE SIMMONS

Captain Kirk had to admit that, actually, there was *one* man who had gone before.

IF GENE SIMMONS STARRED IN THE MOVIE *E.T.*
ONE MAN ACQUIRES AN ENTIRE PLANET
A GENE SIMMONS FILM
G.S.
THE GENETIC SUPERHUMAN
HE IS BOLD.
HE IS HIS OWN HERO.
HE HAS $300,000,000 AND A BIGGER HOUSE THAN YOU.

Gene Simmons once ate a Fabergé egg with bacon and toast.

Eleven percent of the world is left-handed. Gene Simmons couldn't care less about which hand you write with as long as the check is good.

Gene Simmons's property has its own zip code.

If Punxsutawney Phil sees Gene Simmons's shadow, we will not have six more weeks of winter; we will have to pay Gene $5,000 a person to get winter to end.

Gene Simmons craps in the shape of Chuck Norris.

There Was a Hip Rock Star with Seven-Inch Heels

There was a hip rock star, with seven-inch heels.

He had so many dollars, from so many deals.

He didn't need broth, and he didn't need bread;

So he spent it on women, to get them in bed.

Rapunzel let down more than her hair for Gene Simmons.

Gene Simmons beat Arnold Schwarzenegger in a game of thumb wrestling . . . with his penis.

Superman dresses up as Gene Simmons for Halloween every year.

Gene Simmons can get a woman pregnant by staring at her for eight seconds.

Gene Simmons once sang the national anthem at a baseball game and won a Grammy.

When Nike said, "Just Do It," Gene Simmons was way ahead of them.

KISS doesn't have pyrotechnics if Gene Simmons doesn't have gas.

Straight from the Demon's Tongue

"Never fear failure. If you are alive . . . you've won,
no matter what."

—GENE SIMMONS

If you met Gene Simmons what would you ask him?

caN you tEacH ME How to SlEEp witH tHousaNds of WOMEN? (Roger, age 13)

will you give me your pinball machine if i come visit your house? i'll make sure my dad drives a big truck.

(Sam, age 11)

Dude... Do you ever take those sunglasses off?

(James, age 10)

Will you lick my face? (Annie, age 19)

Why do you work in black so much?

(John, age 11)

Mr. Gene Simmons sat on a wall,

Mr. Gene Simmons never will fall.

He owns all the horses and all the king's men,

'Cuz they've been working for him since before they were ten.

IF GENE SIMMONS STARRED
IN THE MOVIE *THE GODFATHER*

All the Power on the Earth...Is Mine!

The God of Thunder

Truth Be Told . . .

Gene cowrote a song with Frank Zappa called "Black Tongue," on the album *Asshole*.

Gene Simmons was taught how to breathe fire by a magician named Amaze-O.

The piano heard in the song "Christine Sixteen" was played by Gene Simmons.

Banging your head against a wall burns 150 calories an hour. Banging Gene Simmons burns 15,000 calories an hour.

Gene Simmons stole Yogi Bear's picnic basket.

Beyoncé's body is too bootylicious for you, but Gene rates her about a 6.

Gene Simmons once held his hand over an open flame till the fire begged for mercy.

The Gene Simmons chess set has one king and thirty-one pawns.

Superman rescued Gene Simmons from atop a burning building. . . . In return, Superman was charged $2,500 for the "Meet and Greet."

I SUGGEST A NEW STRATEGY, R2.

LET THE DEMON WIN.

You Know You're a Gene Simmons Fan When . . .

- You have no photos of you with your tongue inside your mouth.

- Platform boots are a daily accessory.

- You wear more makeup than a Kabuki samurai.

- You walk around stating, "It's good to be *me*."

- Your cod piece has nothing to do with fishing.

- You photograph and catalog the pictures of all of the people you have dated.

Jesus has a Gene Simmons bobblehead.

Gene Simmons can have sex with a woman in seventeen different languages.

When Gene Simmons has a candy bar, it takes off its own wrapper.

When it's the Grim Reaper's time to go, he will be visited by Gene Simmons.

Gene Simmons owns many exotic pets, including the Monkees, the Turtles, and Scorpions.

Neil Diamond's voice can cut records, but Gene Simmons's voice cuts diamonds.

Gene Simmons doesn't get down on himself. Women do that for him.

MC Hammer said, "U Can't Touch This." Gene Simmons did, and now MC Hammer works at Subway.

Straight from the Demon's Tongue

"The sad thing is most people have to check

with someone before they do the things

that make them happy.

We're all passing through;

the least we can do is be happy,

and the only way to do that is by being selfish."

—GENE SIMMONS

When Gene Simmons pokes you on Facebook, it leaves a bruise.

Gene Simmons sold one piece of his chewed gum on eBay . . . for $245,000.

Gene Simmons's house is so big, his maid staff uses MapQuest to find the bathrooms.

Gene Simmons's house is so big, he has a fleet of taxis on duty at all times to get around.

Gene Simmons cleans out his ears with Carrot Top.

Goodyear manufactures steel-belted radial condoms for Gene Simmons.

When Gene Simmons plays Scrabble, everything spells "Gene Simmons."

GENE-TIONARY

Agenda: Having a specific motive or plan.

A-*Gene*-da: Having the specific motive or plan of acquiring money.

Congenital: Of a disease or physical abnormality present from birth.

Con-*Gene*-ital: Of or pertaining to a condition, specifically a superpower or superhuman attribute, present from birth.

Gendarme: A member of the French national police organization constituting a branch of the armed forces with responsibility for general law enforcement.

***Gene*-darme:** A female, in a French police costume, hired by Gene Simmons to "deliver justice," among other things.

Gender: Sex, male or female.

Gene-der: While technically male, a far more superiorly evolved and potent form of male, thus requiring a separate term to differentiate it from ordinary weak human males.

Genealogy: A record or account of the ancestry and descent of a person, family, group, etc. The study of family ancestries and histories.

Gene-alogy: The study/tracing of how many people in your family history slept with Gene Simmons.

General: The highest rank in the military.

Gene-eral: The highest rank in the universe.

Generate: To create or bring into being.

Gene-erate: To create or bring money into being.

Generation: All of the people born and living at about the same time, regarded collectively.

Gene-**eration:** All of the people created from the seed of Gene Simmons, regarded collectively.

Generation X: The generation following the post–World War II baby boom, especially people born in the United States and Canada from the early 1960s to the late 1970s.

Gene-**eration X:** The generation spawned specifically from Gene Simmons over the last four decades.

Generator: A machine designed to make electricity from gas or diesel fuel.

Gene-**erator:** A machine designed to create unlimited renewable energy, from awesomeness.

Generic: Like everything else.

Gene-eric: Unlike *anything* else.

Generous: Willingness to give freely.

Gene-erous: Willingness to give nothing for free.

Genesis: The origin of something.

Gene-esis: The theory that all things were Gene's idea.

Genet: Any of several Old World carnivorous mammals of the genus *Genetta* having grayish or yellowish fur with dark spots and a long ringed tail.

Gene-et: Any of several Old World carnivorous mammals of the genus *Genetta* with a long tongue that can fly and breathe fire and probably banged your girlfriend.

Genetic: The science of heredity, dealing with resemblances and differences of related organisms resulting from the interaction of their genes and the environment.

***Gene*-etic:** The study of how even brief interactions with Gene Simmons can cause sudden and irreversible changes to an organism, despite its genetic predisposition.

Genie: A deity that can and will grant three wishes.

***Gene*-ie:** A deity that can grant unlimited wishes, but it will cost you.

Genitals: Reproductive organs.

***Gene*-itals:** Like genitals, but much, much larger.

Genius: A person of extraordinary intelligence.

***Gene*-ius:** A theoretical level of intelligence unattainable by humans (except one).

Genocide: The eradication of a race or species.

Gene-ocide: A fictional word meaning, in theory, the eradication of the Gene Simmons bloodline, which we all know cannot be done by man or God.

Gentile: A person of non-Jewish descent.

Gene-tile: A person not directly of the Simmons bloodline.

Gentleman: A chivalrous, courteous, or honorable man.

Gene-tleman: Someone more sophisticated than a gentleman, but who can still totally kick a gentleman's ass.

Genuflect: To lower one's body briefly by bending one knee to the ground, typically in worship or as a sign of respect.

Gene-uflect: To lower one's body briefly by bending one knee to the ground, specifically in worship of Gene Simmons.

Geochemistry: The chemistry of the composition and alterations of the solid matter of the earth or a celestial body.

Gene-**ochemistry:** The chemistry of the composition and alterations of the emotions and euphoria of a woman and her body when she thinks about Gene Simmons.

Geocyclic: Of, pertaining to, or illustrating the revolutions of the earth.

Gene-**ocyclic:** Of, pertaining to, or illustrating how most things revolve around Gene Simmons.

Geode: A hollow, usually spheroidal rock with crystals lining the inside wall.

Gene-**ode:** A hollow, usually spheroidal rock with cold, hard cash lining the inside wall.

Geoglossum: Genus of the family Geoglossaceae comprising the earth tongues.

Gene-**oglossum:** Genus of the family Geoglossaceae comprising much longer earth tongues.

Geomancy: Divination by means of lines and figures or by geographic features.

Gene-**omancy:** Divination by means of power, wealth, or by general awesomeness.

Geophagy: The eating of earthy substances, such as clay or chalk, practiced among various peoples as a custom or for dietary or subsistence reasons.

Gene-**ophagy:** The eating of the earth's most expensive substances, such as caviar and other fine foods, practiced by Gene Simmons, because life is too short to eat at McDonald's.

Geophysics: The physics of the earth and its environment, including the physics of fields such as meteorology, oceanography, and seismology.

Gene-**ophysics:** The physics of Gene and his environment, including the physics of such fields as bassology, womenology, and theology of being a Rock God.

Geophyte: A perennial plant that propagates by means of buds below the soil surface.

Gene-**ophyte:** A perennial plant that propagates by means of seducing *all* of the other plants in the field.

Geoponic: Of or relating to agriculture or farming.

Gene-**oponic:** Of or relating to growing your financial portfolio or net worth.

Geothermal: Of or relating to the internal heat of the earth.

***Gene*-othermal:** Of or relating to the internal heat of Gene Simmons, which is 110 times hotter than the internal heat of the earth.

Geotic: Belonging to earth.

***Gene*-otic:** Belonging to Gene.

Legendary: Remarkable enough to be famous; very well-known.

Le-*Gene*-dary: A full tier above legendary, one that legends look up to as superior. So far, only Gene Simmons has achieved le-*Gene*-dary status.

Monogenetic: Involving or controlled by a single gene.

Mono-*Gene*-etic: Involving or controlled by . . . Gene.

Smidgen: A small amount of something.

Smid-*Gene*: What you would get *if* Gene Simmons gave you a portion of something of his. A smid-*Gene* cannot be seen by the human eye.

GENE SIMMONS **EVERY WOMAN ON EARTH** **RICHARD DREYFUSS**

GENE

The terrifying moment you realize they all belong to Gene!

Money, Money, Gene, Gene (Baa Baa Black Sheep)

Money, money, Gene, Gene,

Have you any cash?

Yes, sir, yes, sir,

I've got a stash.

For I am the master,

And I got the dame,

So tough for that little punk

Who lives down the lane.

Marlon Brando pissed off Gene Simmons. The next morning Brando woke up

Straight from the Demon's Tongue

How to Be Gene Simmons

1. Be Gene Simmons.

2. Wonder why all people are not Gene Simmons.

3. Check mirror frequently to make sure you are still Gene Simmons.

4. Under no circumstances allow yourself not to be Gene Simmons.

5. Smile, exhale, relax, everything is going to be OK. . . . You are Gene Simmons.

Gene Simmons once peed his name in the snow, tripling the property value of that land.

Gene Simmons donates a portion of his hair every year. The Kardashians send him a thank-you note.

All of Gene Simmons's kitchen appliances run on diesel.

Gene Simmons can do sign language . . . with his tongue.

Like fine wine, Gene Simmons gets better each year and more valuable.

The Most Interesting Man in the World has all of Gene's albums.

Hey . . . Wait a minute.

How did Gene Simmons's tongue get that long?

He got bit by a frog or a toad.

(Mike, age 6)

He bought a Cow's tongue and glued it on. (Tommy, age 12)

When he was born they pulled him out by it cause they thought it was his leg. (Dave, age 7)

By exercising it in and out a lot.

(Allen, age 11)

An alien came down to earth and gave it to him. (John, age 8)

From kissing a LOT of ladies. (Lori, age 7)

How did Gene Simmons's tongue get that long?

When he was a kid and got in trouble, instead of pulling him around by the ear his mom would yank his tongue and drag him.   (Mike, age 6)

Pure luck.   (Tommy, age 12)

He's been reincarnated from a giraffe.

(Lori, age 9)

It grew from sticking his tongue out at people too many times when he was a kid.   (Dave, age 7)

When you have it your way at Burger King, it's really Gene Simmons's way.

Straight from the Demon's Tongue

On Raising a Daughter

1. Buy a lemon farm.

2. Start discouraging her from dating musicians at a young age by feeding her a lemon every time someone turns on the radio.

3. Live in a 100,000-square-foot mansion; put in a shopping mall, movie theater, roller rink, and anything else she might ever want to leave the house for. When she does leave the house, feed her a lemon.

4. When she meets her first boy, feed her a lemon.

5. When she starts dating, put on the Demon costume, hide in the boyfriend's closet, and pay him a terrifying visit one night early on in the relationship. During that visit, feed him a lemon.

6. When she finds someone you do approve of, on their wedding day, give them the lemon farm as a wedding gift, in case they have a daughter.

Gene Simmons has also saved rock 'n' roll on thirty-one other planets.

Gene Simmons's echo also has a string of hit records.

A typical lightning bolt is two to four inches wide and two miles long and is less shocking than one lick from Gene Simmons's tongue.

Gene Simmons can sing a note so low you'll lose bowel control.

KISS really stands for Knights in Simmons's Service.

Gene Simmons can lick both of his elbows. At the same time.

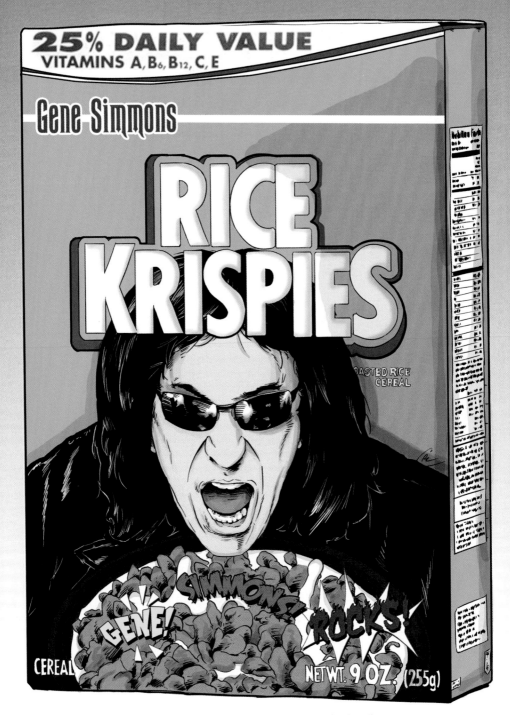

Gene Simmons Rice Krispies do not say, "Snap, Crackle, Pop."
They say, "Gene Simmons Rocks."

Gene Simmons started the Great Chicago Fire.

Rick Springfield wishes he had Jesse's girl. Gene Simmons did . . . twice.

Gene Simmons doesn't own a calendar; he decides what day it is.

Gene Simmons has no character limit on Twitter.

Gene Simmons is smarter than your honor student.

Monthly transfusions of Gene Simmons's blood are what keep Keith Richards alive.

Straight from the Demon's Tongue

"The best things in life are never given; they're earned.

Responsibility, for instance."

—GENE SIMMONS

When Princess Leia said, "I love you," she imagined she was really talking to Gene Simmons.

If you met Gene Simmons what would you ask him?

WHY HE WEARS SO MUCH MAKEUP WHEN HE HAS SUCH A PERFECT FACE. (Raven, age 16)

How long is your tongue and if it was cold would it stick to a pole? (Mary, age 8)

Have you ever kissed a girl? (Brody, age 8)

How long is your tongue and how does it feel to be married to a playmate model? (Sam, age 15)

What's with that hair? (Ellie, age 9)

Flavor Flav wears a clock around his neck, but Gene Simmons wears the Wheel of Fortune.

Superman can leap tall buildings in a single bound. Gene Simmons can buy them.

The tongue is a muscular structure attached to the floor of the mouth. Gene Simmons's tongue is a muscular structure that hits the floor from his mouth.

A Gene Simmons fireball can be seen from space. Astronauts pay the full ticket price.

David Blaine can make a bus disappear. Gene Simmons can make David Blaine disappear.

When Gollum said, "My Precious," he was referring to the Gene Simmons Axe Bass.

Gene Simmons brushes his teeth with wasabi and gargles with propane.

Gene Simmons's testicles have their own weather system and gravitational pull.

China's population explosion is largely due to the fact that Gene tours there. Often.

Donald Trump has Donald Trump hair because Gene Simmons already owns Gene Simmons hair.

Only 55 percent of Americans know the sun is a star, but 100 percent know Gene Simmons is a superstar.

If you met Gene Simmons what would you ask him?

DO YOU like apples? (Mike, age 6)

Did you get zits before you were a rock star?
(Tommy, age 12)

did YOUR MOM ever gROUND YOU FOR USiNg THE F WORd? (Dave, age 7)

How many boobs have you touched? (Allen, age 11)

Do you wear your KISS costume on Christmas? (Lori, age 7)

How do you go to the bathroom when you have that Demon costume on? (Jake, age 8)

Peter Peter Pumpkin Eater

Peter, Peter, pumpkin eater,

Had a wife and couldn't keep her.

Gene Simmons went and rang her bell,

So she told Peter, "Go to Hell."

Gene Simmons flew United Airlines. Shortly thereafter, a United flight attendant suggested the slogan "Flying the Friendly Skies."

Paul Masson says,
"We will sell no wine before its time."

When Gene Simmons was young, his Big Wheel was a Humvee.

Gene Simmons was once asked to leave a restaurant when he misunderstood the phrase "Please leave the server a tip."

If harnessed, one of Gene Simmons's testicles could power the city of Las Vegas for 187 years.

A Gene Simmons idea converts to money so fast it produces a sonic boom.

Gene Simmons's cup is never half empty.

Truth Be Told . . .

Whenever Gene Simmons entered into a relationship
with a woman, one of the first things he did was show her
his infamous Polaroid book, which contained photos of
the countless women he'd been with. He did this so that
a prospective girlfriend could see what he's about so there
were no secrets from his side of the relationship.

The Playboy Mansion rents Gene Simmons's tongue for its annual Slip 'N Slide contest.

The IRS pays taxes to Gene Simmons.

Gene Simmons's gold card is actually made of platinum.

Banks need to fill out applications to see if they are credit-worthy enough to lend money to Gene Simmons.

When Gene Simmons leaves the country, the US dollar drops in value.

Gene Simmons's Escalade has a walk-in glove compartment.

Straight from the Demon's Tongue

"Whoever said

'Money can't buy you love'

obviously was not

making enough money."

—GENE SIMMONS

George Lucas was thinking about what a lightsaber would look like while Gene Simmons was using the urinal next to him. Gene now gets royalties from George Lucas.

Gene Simmons is my father!!!

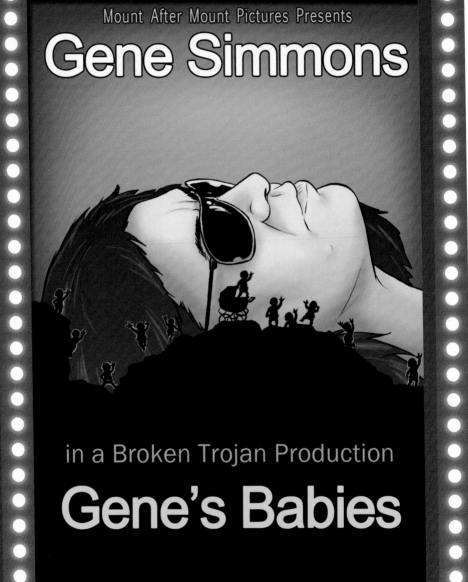

Truth Be Told . . .

Gene Simmons taught public school in Spanish Harlem while moonlighting for his music career.

He departed from traditional English curriculum by using Spider-Man comic books as teaching aids instead of classic literature.

Gene briefly managed Liza Minnelli in the eighties.

Jack Sprat

Jack Sprat could eat no fat.

His wife could eat no lean.

It's for the best because that left

Yet one more girl for Gene.

Gene Simmons once made an onion cry.

Gene Simmons gives Red Bull wings.

Gene Simmons's hair is waterproof, foolproof, and bulletproof.

Gene Simmons *is* the horse your girlfriend rode in on.

If the population of China walked past you in single file, the line would never end because of the rate of reproduction. The same occurs with girls in line to meet Gene Simmons.

If Gene Simmons farts and you smell it, you owe him $126.

Sesame Street can't afford to be brought to us by the letter *G* or *S*.

Next to the thermostat in Gene Simmons's mansion, there is a larger thermostat that controls the weather over his property.

Gene Simmons's ego is so big two black holes have been sucked into it.

When Gene Simmons looks in a mirror, his own reflection can't take his eyes off him.

Gene Simmons can intimidate water into boiling.

Gene Simmons routinely beats Donald Trump at Monopoly.

Gene Simmons uses Steven Tyler to pick the pubes out of his teeth.

McDonald's once wanted to add a Gene Simmons toy for children, but it brought the price of the Happy Meal up to $86.

If Gene Simmons had a dollar for every time he . . . Oh, wait, he does.

A Rubik's Cube has 43,252,003,274,489,856,000 possible configurations. That's two fewer than Gene Simmons has sexual positions.

Genie, Genie, Quite Contrary

Genie, Genie, string bikini,

I wish I had your dough.

With buxom belles and chic hotels,

A life I'll never know.

Hot dogs say, "I wish I were an Oscar Mayer wiener." Everyone else says, "I wish I were Gene Simmons's wiener."

Having sex at least once per week can lower a man's risk of heart disease by 30 percent, stroke by 50 percent, and diabetes by 40 percent. It has also been shown that men with an active sex life are more likely to live past eighty years. Gene Simmons will outlive every human being on the planet.

When Gene Simmons licks a stamp, the postage doubles.

The wife of Jaguar's CEO slept with Gene Simmons. It was her detailed confession to her husband that gave him the idea for the twelve-cylinder engine.

Gene Simmons has honorary doctorates in love from every university.

Gene Simmons can do push-ups with his tongue.

You Know You're a Gene Simmons Fan When . . .

- You thought Gene deserved an Oscar for his acting in the movie *Extract.*

- You're disappointed with the length of your tongue.

- As a kid you spent $80 at a carnival trying to win a $10 poster of *KISS Meets the Phantom of the Park.*

- You draw Demon makeup on your kid's dolls.

- You have taken up breathing fire as a hobby.

- Your entire wardrobe is black leather.

Gene Simmons owns all of the nudist colonies in the world.

Gene Simmons can set fire on fire.

Gene Simmons could get a chick in solitary confinement.

When Gene Simmons talks, E. F. Hutton listens.

There is a town in Pennsylvania named Intercourse and it has only one road, and that road leads to a home owned by Gene Simmons.

When Gene Simmons was born, the doctor held him up and said, "It's alive! It's alive!"

Gene Simmons's Bucket List

1. Win an Oscar for Best Actor in an epic remake of *Gone with the Wind.*

2. Have his Beverly Hills property recognized as the fifty-first US state.

3. Outlive Mick Jagger *and* Keith Richards.

4. Invent a time machine, go back to 1977, and save Elvis.

5. Purchase Mount Rushmore and have his face added.

6. Be recognized as the Eighth Wonder of the World.

7. Have his portrait hanging in the Louvre.

8. Race Paul McCartney on a Big Wheel.

9. Rent a bounce house for his hundredth birthday and bounce around with Shannon Tweed, Oprah, Madonna, Hillary Clinton, Queen Elizabeth, and Betty Rubble.

Straight from the Demon's Tongue

"Before I ever knew what the word *entrepreneur* was, I realized in America and in the Western part of the world in general, you are given the opportunity to be whatever you want to be.

And that is all anyone should ever expect from the capitalist system.

The rest is up to you.

It's up to you to educate yourself.

It's up to you to learn speaking skills and people skills.

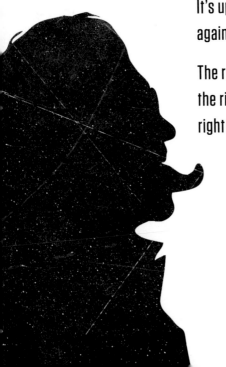

It's up to you to try (and usually fail, but to try again) all sorts of ventures.

The rest is a combination of hard work, being at the right place at the right time . . . with the right thing . . . oh, yes . . . and more hard work."

—**GENE SIMMONS**

What was Gene Simmons before he was a rock star?

He was either a normal person like me or an acrobat, not like me. (Torrey, age 8)

A kid that farted lightning balls. (Jeremy, age 9)

A kid whose mom probably yelled at him a lot. (PJ, age 9)

A kid that ran around dressed up like Dracula. (Julia, age 7)

HE WAS A BOY THAT DID VERY SILLY THINGS AND MADE PEOPLE WONDER ABOUT HIM. I THINK PEOPLE STILL WONDER ABOUT HIM EVEN THOUGH HE'S NOT A KID ANYMORE.

(Betty, age 11)